Beautiful Nonsense

Molly Murray

BookLeaf Publishing

India | USA | UK

Presentation by *BookLeaf Publishing*

Web: www.bookleafpub.com

E-mail: info@bookleafpub.com

ISBN: 9789360941369

First edition 2024

*My mother - who inspired my love of
Beautiful Nonsense.*

*Fawn - that whispers the words I need to
hear.*

ACKNOWLEDGEMENT

I never felt the need to show anyone my poetry.
On a dare, I was tasked with writing one on the
spot.
I wrote Breathing.
Thank you.
For seeing things in me
that I can't always see myself.

PREFACE

I've written poetry off and on for years.
In the back of notebooks, on scraps of paper, a napkin.
Sometimes I've kept them, sometimes I've lost them.
It's always been an act inspired in the moment. When there is something so striking that it can't be captured in any other way.
Only recently have I shared any of my poetry and was encouraged that other people could feel those moments in time through them.

Beautiful Nonsense

My mother was a collector of jars.
She filled them with Beautiful Nonsense.

Dice and old mismatched game pieces,
pretty pictures cut from packages,
sea glass found in forgotten baskets
tucked away on the back shelf of an antique
store.
Old partially used bobbins of red thread.

Beautiful Nonsense is a moment -
that fills your soul with joy.

Each piece was a slice of time,
out of time
and carefully placed into the jar.
Each one was chosen because it filled her soul
with a love so joyous she couldn't bear to not try
and hold onto it.

My mother's house was filled with Beautiful
Nonsense
moments forever preserved in time.

Sunflowers in January

Bringing Sunflowers in January,
not knowing that I needed them.

Knowing that I needed them.

Sought out,
at the wrong time of year.

Right before it all

F
  E
    L
     L

        A
          P
            A
              R
                T

My shoes tell my stories

The Shiny Black Buckle shoes
lost in the whirlpool,
that took me so fast
and tried to keep all of me.
But only kept my shoes.

Doc Martens
bought abroad.
too masculine for my grandfather to approve.
It's not what a young lady ought to wear.
I was his least favourite grandchild,
I was his only grandchild.
But I liked the smell of the leather,
and the bright yellow stitching.

The Combat Boots
that only came in men's sizes,
blending in to look like everyone else.
A means to an end.

Winter Boots
That never fit
but they were warm.
Only ever lasting for a single season.

The shoes I left behind at the party,

because I forgot they existed.

Dancing Shoes
when I gave up waiting for others to find my
happiness
and started seeking out my own joy.

Gray Boots
Just my size but far too expensive.
Far above my class.
That looked great
and made me feel pretty.
but were unnecessary.
Bought for me in an expression of love.

My Bare Feet
that dig in the dirt,
touch the soft grass,
feel the mud squish around them,
walk along the concrete.
My feet that climb trees,
work & play equally hard.

That get decorated.
Sometimes on purpose
sometimes on accident...

They ground me to where I am -
right now.

Tulsa Oklahoma

A large pickup truck sits alone
in an empty parking lot.
A trailer twice its size attached
to the hitch.

In the middle,
carefully strapped down,
a bright red tricycle.

Coffee Cups

It doesn't matter which coffee cup you choose.
They all hold coffee.

But it matters which coffee cup you choose.

One that sits between your legs as you turn the
pages.

That fits in your hand,
just right.

Steam rising.
Inhaling the scent.

The cup that speaks to you that morning
or reminds you of -
a time,
a place,
a person.

The one with the chip
from moving across the country.
or the gifted one.

The first cup

you bought for yourself.

The cup is as important
as that first sip.

Preacher Man

The preacher man sits,
carefully wrapping his cardboard shoes in duct
tape.
Savouring the moment of warmth,
in the entryway between buildings.
He stops.
Illuminated by the soft backlight.
I see him kneel to pray.

Ponds and puppy dog tails

Walking along the bank of the pond.
You still wobble
but have been walking confidently for a year or
more now.
"Watch your step," I say

The grass mushes under our feet,
ground shifting strangely,
creating unexpected sinkholes.

The image of you falling
into the pond
slips in and out of my mind.
While we wander,
looking for bugs and colourful rocks.

I carry the baby on my hip
and a bag of found treasures.

I reach out to take your hand,
grasping your little fingers awkwardly in mine.

Just as the ground
slips away
from under you.

Lifting you up
as you fall downward.

Before your toes even touch the water
you are back safely,
on solid ground.

Continuing the adventure.
Without ever knowing,
that for a moment,
you were almost
lost.

Bone collector

We are a collection of moments.
It doesn't need to be perfect.
Most of the time it isn't.

Beauty is found in-between the lines of living
life.
Found moments.
Unexpected events.
Joy in nonsense.
Sorrow in growth.

When I'm lying in my grave,
what do I want remembered of me?

Let the life I lived,
speak for me.

Next to you

Walking through the slush.
Sometimes we walk together
under the Christmas lights hung through the
trees in the park.

Other times the sidewalk narrows,
I go first.
you go first.

There isn't a need to discuss when
we part ways,
or when we come back together.

We navigate the walk.
Feeling each other's presence.

The snow falls gently,
tiny shimmering flakes
catching the city lights.

The magick you bring to the table

Imagine taking each first bite,
as if it were the most exquisite thing
you've ever encountered.

So much more than sustenance.
The physical representation of love,
meant to be consumed.
With no expectation of reciprocity.

The sharing of food is magick.
Food is the spiritual act of love.
The joy of giving and the joy of receiving,
is all that can be offered in a meal.

The food we eat connects us,
to the soil, the sower, the harvester.
Devotion is the spiritual act of commitment for a
specific purpose.

There is food to celebrate abundance,
of births, of deaths, of milestones.
Creation of community lives in the heart of the
kitchen.

There is magick in the serving of food.
It doesn't matter if the meal is
only for you
or for many.

Each.and.every.bite.is.magick.

All food is sacred.
Savor that first bite.
Prepared by hands,
or ordered in.

More than nourishment of the body.
This ritual,
This prayer,
Will never be repeated.
This sacred act can only be performed once.
And yet,
can be performed many times.

Each meal,
A holy sacrament.

Breathing

Breathing in
as you,
breathe out.

Sharing the soul scoop,
literally, the breath of life.
Taking in this moment,
just as it is.

And for that moment,

there isn't anything else.

Unrequited Love

Once upon a time,
I had a boyfriend.
He wasn't good for me,
But he was my first,
So I hung on much longer than I should have.

He had a brother.
who noticed
I only ate the orange M&M's.

Who carefully picked out all the other colours
from the bowl,
leaving me with only my favourites.

He never said anything,
just quietly left me that small gift of love.

He killed himself the following week.

I never got to thank him.

Mazatlan

A man greets me on the beach.
He gestures that he wants to look
at my book.

I quickly look at my page number,
and hand it to him.

Taking a seat next to me,
with much to say.

No habla Espanol I reply.
He continues…
The only word in English is "listen."

He carefully tears the page out.
the next page,
yet unread,
the start of a new chapter.

Gently, he folds it,
places it in his pocket,
hands me my book,

And walks away.

The clock that doesn't work

A beautiful wooden clock.
Handcrafted, with tender care.
A beautiful wooden clock,
that doesn't work.

Hands ticking across its face,
always between 6:25 and 6:45.

There is never enough time - it moves too fast
it also, moves slowly.

Each moment, a lifetime,
in and of itself.

Whole lives lived in the ticks
between 6:25 and 6:45.

Silent prayer

Every morning I start a fire.
Warming the house,
after the cool-down over the winter night.
I kneel,
encouraging the flames with my breath.
Glowing coals slowly coming back to life.

The spark catches
slowly at first,
crackling in that way that fire does
as it works its way up between the bark.

I take a moment,
to express my gratitude.

Into the Woods

There was a coffee shop in the woods.
Just a little cabin,
mostly unnoticed.

Poetry lined the shelves
and instruments hung on the wall.
There was bed,
tucked away in the back.
In case you needed a place to stay that night
but you had to know it was there.

Unwritten rules.
You just knew
or you didn't,
and then you didn't stay long.

This was a place of sanctuary,
community.

Whoever was closest to the counter
made the coffee.
You locked the doors if you
were the last to leave.

There was no expectation

that when you finished your coffee,
you moved on with your day.

Spending long evenings,
in conversation
or art
or silence.

I never appreciated how much that place
formed my view,
of what life could look like.

Finders Keepers

There is poetry in found moments.
The way legs entangle as you sleep.
A beautiful, unexpected gift.
The way someone looks at you,
or says your name,
full of love.

When the light shines through the curtain,
in just the right way.
Spontaneous laughter,
emotions so overwhelming, you tear up.
In the simple way,
you hold hands.

Moments,
That means nothing out of context.
But right then,
They mean everything.

Dead Air

Sometimes,
I hear music playing.
Like a distant radio.
Just as I drift off to sleep.

It takes the place,
of where
you should to be .

Five Minutes

I need five minutes,
to be hopeless.

Just five minutes.

To let go.

with no judgment,
or assurances,
or advice,

Five minutes to feel the things I need to feel.

That someday,
there might be nothing there for me to fall back
on.

That maybe it will hurt a little less,
if I don't fall quite so far.

Then I will wipe my face
and continue on.

Finding myself again

I always wanted to dance,
I got tired of asking.
I found myself again
on the dance floor.

I use the nice things,
not fearing that it won't be perfect.
Instead,
enjoying them thoroughly.

Leaving behind what depletes me,
Embracing that which replenishes my soul.
Finding renewal in the everyday acts.
Lighting a candle.
Making the mundane sacred.

Not later,
or it could have been
in another time or place.

This is my reality.
accepting that I can't know
what happens next.

Becoming comfortable
with myself.

Frosted Windows

The feel of the cool floor on my feet
as I quietly get up,
to put the coffee on.

Sounds of the house slowly waking up,
shifting in bed,
light shining through the windows
peeking just over the mountains.
Eggs sizzling in the cast iron.

Looking through the frosted trees at the sunrise
on a New Year's Day.

9 789360 941369